Christmas 2011

Dearest Lynette

The 1st Vision is truly
from God. The Spirit has
whispered it is true to me.
Love you Dear Friend

Kate

A DAY LIKE NO OTHER

JOSEPH SMITH *and* THE FIRST VISION

Scot Facer Proctor

Some mornings are very special. The light and fog play with each other in a wonderful way showing us what sunbeams really look like. It was such a morning one October when I had my camera with me at the Joseph Smith Farm near Palmyra, New York.

Will you come with me and take a walk together in this sacred place? I will tell you about a day like no other.

Our story begins with an obscure farm boy named Joseph Smith who, though he had a most common name, would have a most uncommon experience.

He lived in a time when people believed that God no longer spoke directly to His children, that the heavens were now silent.

In this snug little cabin, his large family of three sisters and six brothers all crowded around the fire, where they learned from the Bible by night and then worked very hard on their farm by day.

When they first bought their
100-acre farm, it was a dense forest of ancient trees, some so
huge that an eight-foot crosscut could hardly saw through them.
Yet they could not farm the land, unless they cut down the trees and
then pulled out the enormous stumps that were left behind.

This was extremely hard work for a boy so young, and
Joseph became strong.

If you had been on their farm, you would have smelled sawdust
and smoke and heard the cracking and felling of trees.

oseph's mother, Lucy, said that every where they looked the result of their hard work smiled upon them. A more pleasant place she could not imagine with its orchards, maple trees for sugaring and trim fields and split-rail fences.

On the frontiers of America, many boys spent their time just like Joseph—felling trees and building fences—but something extraordinary was about to happen to Joseph that would set him apart from all others.

The extraordinary thing began with questions.

"What church should I join? Where can I learn about God in a way I can trust? Who can tell me the truth?"

He cleared the land and these questions weighed upon him. He rested against the trunk of a tree, and he had the same thoughts. He was wondering about the things of God.

here could he find the answers? Nobody in his family could answer them.

He had been taught the scriptures and he believed them, but all about him people seemed to understand them differently.

Joseph worked around the farm and walked out among the woods, wondering: "Who will guide me?"

The preachers round about Palmyra all claimed to have the answers Joseph sought. They argued with each other and each sounded his own message with great excitement hoping to gain converts. For Joseph it was a war of words and a contest of opinions, all strife and noise.

He said, "Who of all these parties are right; or, are they all wrong together? If any of them be right, which is it, and how shall I know it?"

Joseph knew that God could not be the Author of such great confusion. He knew that if God had a church on the earth, it wouldn't be split up into pieces.

**Y**oung Joseph
came out to these fields at night. The stars were

clear and beautiful, and he could see the

Milky Way Galaxy. He wondered why the sun,

moon and stars were so perfect in their order,

but why people—including him—seemed to be

so very confused about religion.

Though the water
from this well on his farm was clear
and fresh, it could not quench his thirst.

He was thirsty to know the things
of God and drink from the living water
only Jesus could give.

Joseph decided
it was impossible for a person as young as
he was to come to any certain conclusion who
was right and who was wrong.

Then one day Joseph was reading in the Bible, in the Book of James, and came to this passage: "If any of you lack wisdom, let him ask of God, that giveth to all men liberally, and upbraideth not; and it shall be given him. But let him ask in faith, nothing wavering."

This scripture seemed to enter with great force into every feeling of Joseph's heart. Could this be the answer he was looking for—to ask God Himself?

ever did any

passage of scripture come with more power to the heart of

man than this did at this time to mine," Joseph said.

"I reflected on it again and again, knowing that if any person

needed wisdom from God, I did; for how to act I did

not know, and unless I could get more wisdom than I then

had, I would never know."

oseph had been
taught from the Bible that God was the same yesterday,
today and forever. He had learned that God was
no respecter of persons and that one prayer was just as
important to God as any other.

sk of God—
he will give liberally," he thought. "Ask in
faith, nothing wavering."

Even though Joseph was only a farm
boy, this knowledge gave him great confidence.

nowing his farm well,

Joseph thought of a special place in a grove of trees

where he could go to be alone and make an attempt to pray

to God, for he had never as yet tried to pray out loud.

It was on the morning of a beautiful, clear day,

early in the spring of 1820.

This would be the day like no other.

Joseph walked
across these fields away from his
family's cabin. His shoes and his pant legs
probably became very wet from the
heavy spring dew on the grasses and weeds.

He had to cross this little stream as he headed to the grove. He probably knew this creek well and had played in it and followed its course many times. He may have caught frogs and crawdads and watched skeeters dart around on the water.

Now he had other things on his mind.

Was Joseph's

heart pounding as he came closer to the woods?

Was he a little hungry that morning?

Did he tell one of his brothers where he was going?

Do you think he might have passed a

crow perched on the fence?

What did he plan to say in his prayer?

Joseph made sure
he walked far away from the road.
He didn't want any one to see him when
he knelt down and prayed. He
just wanted to be alone with God.

He walked deep
into the woods, going past thick undergrowth
and through lots of dead leaves.

e walked
by very tall trees— many over a

hundred feet high.

The forest was

filled with the sounds of birds

and squirrels.

Joseph knew this place well.

e looked around
to make sure he was alone, then knelt down to
pray and offer up the desires of his heart.

Then suddenly, the unexpected.

He heard a stick crack behind him. He jumped
up to see who was there. He saw no one.
He tried to pray again but his tongue grew thick
and he could not speak. Thick darkness
gathered all around him.

He was seized
by some power which entirely
overcame him, being attacked by "an actual
being from the unseen world" who did
not want Joseph to have his prayer answered.

Joseph cried out
to God with all of his heart to be delivered
from this enemy who held him bound.

At that moment of greatest alarm,
when Joseph felt like he was doomed to sudden
destruction, a glorious light began to appear.

saw a pillar
of light exactly over my head," Joseph said,
"above the brightness of the sun,
which descended gradually until it fell upon me."

"It no sooner appeared than I found myself
delivered from the enemy which held me bound."

I saw two Personages, whose brightness and glory defy all description, standing above me in the air. One of them spake unto me, calling me by name and said, pointing to the other—'Joseph, This is my Beloved Son. Hear Him!'"

Heavenly Father and His Son, Jesus Christ stood before Joseph Smith and they were talking personally to him.

With that one glimpse, Joseph now knew more about God than all the teachers of religion in the world, and it was only the beginning.

Composing himself, Joseph asked which of all the churches was right and which one he should join.

Jesus said he was to join none of them. "They draw near to me with their lips, but their hearts are far from me."

The prophets from ancient times have always been given visions of the eternities. They have been told what their role would be. It would be no different with this young prophet. Joseph was told that he would be an instrument in bringing the true church of Jesus Christ back to the earth.

He was filled with the love of God. His prayer had been answered in a glorious way and his mind was now settled as to what to do.

Though Joseph
would be hated and persecuted for saying that he
had seen a vision, he would say, "I had actually
seen a light, and in the midst of that light
I saw two Personages, and they did in reality speak
to me. I knew it, and I knew that God knew it,
and I could not deny it."

Joseph Smith would go
on from this now Sacred Grove to become a mighty prophet.

He would become an instrument in the Lord's

Hands to bring back the priesthood authority and keys,

and to organize the Church of Jesus Christ,

just as in the days when Jesus was on the earth.

od had

again called a prophet.

The silence of centuries was broken.

This was a day like no other.

Meridian Publishing
PO Box 94
Fairfax Station, VA 22039-0094

Order information: www.intothegrove.com

This is not an official publication of
The Church of Jesus Christ of Latter-day Saints.

Printed in Reynosa, Mexico.
November 2009

ISBN 978-1-934537-08-4